STAR WARS™
THE CLONE WARS™

LEVEL 2

SCHOLASTIC

Adapted by: Paul Shipton

Publisher: Jacquie Bloese

Editors: Patricia Reilly, Emma Grisewood

Cover layout: Mo Choy

Designer: Mo Choy

Picture research: Osha Hufton

Photo credits:
Cover & pages 4, 5, 6, 7, 9, 11, 13, 14, 15, 17, 18, 19, 20, 22, 23, 24, 25, 27, 28, 29, 30, 31, 34, 35, 37, 38, 39, 40, 41, 42, 44, 46, 47, 48 & 49: Courtesy of Lucasfilm Ltd.
Pages 50 & 51: K. Winter/AFP/Getty Images; Lucasfilm Ltd.
Pages 52 & 53: Nasa/AFP/Getty Images; S. Ponomarey/PA; Nasa/Alamy; Nasa.

Published by Scholastic Ltd. 2009

Mary Glasgow Magazines (Scholastic Ltd)
Euston House
24 Eversholt Street
London
NW1 1DB

Printed in Singapore. This edition printed in 2010.

CONTENTS

THE REPUBLIC

The Republic is a group of planets in space. In this world, people travel in big spaceships and talk to each other using holograms. But the Republic has problems too …

OBI-WAN KENOBI

Obi-Wan is a strong Jedi Master. Like Anakin, he fights against the enemies of the Republic. He was Anakin's teacher.

AHSOKA

is Anakin's Padawan. A Padawan is a student who is learning to be a Jedi Knight.

YODA

is a very old Jedi – he is over 800 years old. He is small, but the Force is very strong in him.

ANAKIN SKYWALKER

is a Jedi Knight. Jedi can use the Force. The Force is a strange energy in all things. They do not use guns – they fight with lightsabers.

PADMÉ AMIDALA
was once a Queen on the planet of Naboo. Now she lives on Coruscant. She is a Senator of the Republic. The Senators decide on all the important things.

SUPREME CHANCELLOR PALPATINE
is a very important man in the Republic. The Chancellor is the leader of all the Senators.

MACE WINDU
is one of the Jedi's most important leaders.

PLACES

CORUSCANT
is in the centre of the Republic. The whole planet is one enormous city. The Senate is on Coruscant. The Senate is where the Senators and Chancellor meet. The Jedi Temple is here too.

Coruscant

CHRISTOPHSIS
is a planet in the Republic. The enemies of the Republic want it for themselves.

TETH
is a planet outside the Republic. Anakin and Ahsoka come here to find Jabba's son.

TATOOINE
is a planet far outside the Republic. Tatooine is important for the Republic. The Republic's ships need to pass through its air space to get to other planets.

THE ENEMIES OF THE REPUBLIC

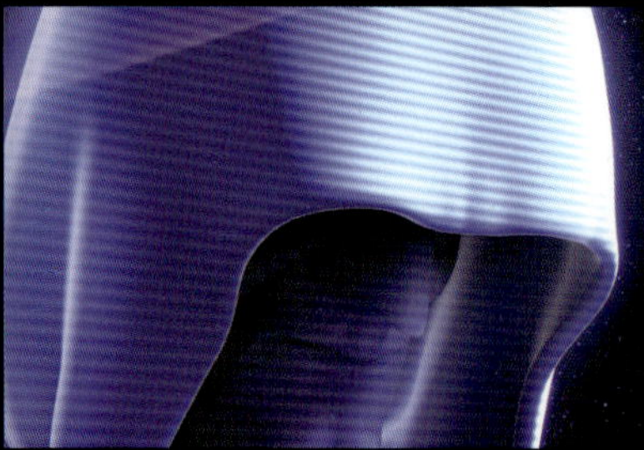

DARTH SIDIOUS

is as strong as any Jedi, but he is a Sith – he follows the dark side of the Force. Sidious thinks the Republic is weak and must end.

COUNT DOOKU

was once a Jedi, but he became a Sith. Now he follows the orders of Darth Sidious in his plan to end the Republic.

ASAJJ VENTRESS

turned to the dark side of the Force, and now she works for Dooku. She is very dangerous and fights with two lightsabers.

GENERAL LOATHSOM

wants to end the Republic with his droid armies.

THE HUTTS

JABBA THE HUTT

is the boss on the planet of Tatooine. He is very unhappy when his son Rotta disappears.

ZIRO

is Jabba's uncle. He lives on Coruscant now.

CLONES ...

Clones are living copies of a person. They are people.

Captain Rex

CAPTAIN REX AND COMMANDER CODY

are both leaders in the Republic's army of clone troopers. The Republic 'made' this army to fight for it. Captains and commanders give orders to the other troopers. The Jedi are the generals – the leaders – of all the clone troopers.

Commander Cody

... AND DROIDS

Droids are like thinking, moving computers. Both the Republic and its enemies use droids for lots of different jobs. Tanks are a kind of droid.

C-3PO (THREEPIO)

is Amidala's droid. He can speak over six million languages, but he's not very good in battle!

R2-D2 (ARTOO)

is a small droid, but he is a good fighter. He was once on Amidala's ship, but he became Anakin's droid. He is very good with computers.

Tank droids

PROLOGUE

Coruscant was the centre of the Republic. One building there stood taller than all others on the planet. This was the Jedi Temple, home to the Jedi leaders. Their job was very important – to keep the Republic and all its planets safe.

But the Republic had many enemies. They thought the Republic was weak. One of them, Count Dooku, was now attacking Republic planets with his army of droids. The Republic fought back with thousands of clone troopers, but they needed help from the Jedi.

But now there was a problem. Yoda was talking to Mace Windu. The two looked very different – Mace was tall and Yoda was little and green – but they were both important Jedi.

'We must speak to Obi-Wan and Anakin,' said Mace.

At that moment Obi-Wan Kenobi and Anakin Skywalker were fighting droids on the planet of Christophsis.

Mace and Yoda sent a hologram* message to a Republic ship near Christophsis.

'We have an important message for Obi-Wan,' said Mace.

'He's on the planet,' answered the ship's leader. 'But the weather is bad. We can't send any messages to him.'

There was no time to wait. Yoda said, 'We are sending somebody with orders for Obi-Wan.'

* People's faces appear in a hologram message.

CHAPTER 1
A new student

Far away in Crystal City, on Christophsis, Anakin was ready to fight again.

'The droids are back!' he shouted to his clone troopers. 'More enemy droids are coming – lots more.'

'I told you that battle was too easy,' cried Obi-Wan. 'It was a mistake to send our ship away.'

'That wasn't my idea!' Anakin said quickly to his old Master*.

He turned to the leader of the clone troopers and shouted, 'Captain Rex, you and your men follow me!'

They ran to the side of the street. The other troopers and their leader, Commander Cody, stayed with Obi-Wan. The Jedi's lightsaber was in his hand. This was going to be a hard battle. Lots of droids were coming. They were all strong and dangerous, and they all had guns.

Obi-Wan waited and then shouted, 'Now!'

The clone troopers ran at the droids. The sound was terrible as the droids started firing their guns.

But Obi-Wan was too fast for them. He started cutting at the droids with his lightsaber. First one fell, then another.

* Jedi students call their teacher and other important Jedi 'Master'.

But it was no good; there were just too many. When one fell, another took its place.

'Where's General Skywalker? Why hasn't he attacked?' shouted Cody above the sounds of battle.

'Don't worry!' answered Obi-Wan. 'He knows the plan.'

Behind the other droids, three big insect droids ran on their long legs. Their red lights looked like scary eyes.

Now Anakin and his men were behind the enemy droids.

'Follow me,' Anakin told Rex.

He jumped on top of one of the big droids. Before it could do anything, the Jedi pushed his lightsaber into it. The droid fell, but Anakin did not stop. Moments later, he destroyed the second one.

Now Obi-Wan and his men were in front of the enemy droids and Anakin was behind them. The droids didn't know which way to attack. The battle was going well for the Republic army now. Their plan was working!

One of the battle droids talked to a hologram of their leader, General Loathsom. Like Count Dooku, Loathsom wanted to end the Republic.

'We cannot get past them,' the droid said.

'Then move back,' Loathsom ordered. 'We will use the shield.'

Anakin and Obi-Wan watched as the enemy started to leave. Both men knew that the battle was not over. Soon the droids were going to attack again.

Suddenly there was a sound from above. They looked up – it was a Republic ship!

'Help has arrived,' smiled Obi-Wan.

The door of the ship opened. The Jedi Knights were surprised when a young girl walked out.

'Who are you?' asked Anakin.

'I'm Ahsoka. Master Yoda sent me with a message. You must return to the Jedi Temple immediately,' she said.

'We've got our own problems here,' said Anakin.

'Yes, we were trying to call for help,' said Obi-Wan, 'but we couldn't send a message.'

Ahsoka had a holoprojector* with her. 'Why don't you use our ship to send a message to Master Yoda?'

Anakin did not want to say it, but this was a good idea. Moments later, they were looking at a hologram of Yoda.

'We need help,' Obi-Wan told him. 'We cannot leave the planet – there are too many droids here.'

'We will send help,' answered Yoda.

Then enemy fighters started attacking the Republic ship and the hologram picture slowly disappeared. The fighters were small battleships and they could attack quickly.

'We must fight here for a while longer,' Anakin told the others.

Obi-Wan smiled at Ahsoka. 'I'm Obi-Wan Kenobi, your new Master. You must be my Padawan. I'm happy to be your teacher.'

A Padawan was a Jedi student who worked and studied with a Jedi Knight.

* A holoprojector is like a mobile phone, but you can see a hologram of the person who you are talking to.

But Ahsoka said, 'Master Yoda gave me different orders. I am Master Skywalker's Padawan.'

'What?' cried Anakin. 'I didn't want a Padawan. *Obi-Wan* did!'

'We'll talk about this later,' said Obi-Wan. 'Take Ahsoka with you until then.'

Ahsoka followed Anakin as he went to speak to Captain Rex. The clone leader was speaking to his troopers about the next attack.

'Who's the girl?' Rex asked.

'I'm Master Skywalker's Padawan,' Ahsoka answered.

'It's a mistake,' said Anakin. He was a bit angry.

'No – no mistake. I'm your student, Skyguy*,' Ahsoka said.

'What did you call me?' Anakin said. 'Don't get snippy with me!'

Suddenly, a big ball of orange energy appeared on the other side of the city.

'What's that?' Ahsoka asked.

'The enemy have got an energy shield,' Rex said. 'It will be almost impossible to stop them now.'

Ahsoka was frightened for a moment. Was she ready for this?

'Yes!' she told herself. 'I must show Anakin what I can do!'

Minutes later, the Jedi and the clone leaders were looking at a hologram map of the city. Obi-Wan pointed to one part. 'The shield generator is somewhere around here. The shield will be very big now. All the droids are behind it and they are coming closer and closer.'

Ahsoka spoke. 'The shield's a problem … so let's destroy it.' She pulled Anakin's arm. 'Let's go!'

* Ahsoka calls Anakin 'Skyguy' as a joke because his name is 'Skywalker'.

Anakin followed his Padawan, but then she asked, 'What now?'

'You mean you don't know, Snips*?'

But Anakin was smiling – he had a plan! Quickly he found a big piece of wood.

'Hide under this!' he told Ahsoka. Together they moved slowly to the energy shield.

'This is stupid!' said Ahsoka.

'No, it isn't,' said Anakin. 'The shield went over us a few moments ago.'

They could hear a loud sound – something was coming. Anakin looked out and opened his mouth in surprise. There were lots and lots of tank droids, and they were all coming towards them …

* Anakin calls Ahsoka 'Snips' because he thinks she is sometimes 'snippy'. A 'snippy' person is sometimes rude in a funny way.

CHAPTER 2
Surrender!

Obi-Wan, Rex and the troopers were fighting wave after wave of battle droids. One droid held a trooper by the neck against the wall. Obi-Wan ran to it and – *WHOOSH!* – he used his lightsaber to cut off one of the droid's arms. It dropped the trooper and attacked Obi-Wan. But the Jedi used the energy of the Force to push it back.

The rest of the troopers were fighting hard, but there were too many droids.

'Rex!' shouted Obi-Wan. 'Move your men back to the big guns! I'll stay here.'

'But …' Rex couldn't leave his leader alone with the enemy.

'That is an order, Captain Rex!' shouted Obi-Wan.

As the clones followed Rex, more and more droids were around Obi-Wan. His lightsaber moved fast, and droid after droid fell. But more were coming. And Obi-Wan could hear another sound – droid tanks!

'I hope Anakin and Ahsoka find that generator soon,' he thought.

* * *

Anakin and Ahsoka watched as the last of the tanks went past them.

Ahsoka was excited. 'They didn't see us!'

Now they were near the shield generator. It was in the middle of a field.

'Come on!' cried Ahsoka.

'No! Wait!'

Anakin's words came too late. When Ahsoka put a foot on the field, something started to move – something under the grass. It was a droid, and it wasn't alone. There was a small army of them to keep the shield generator safe. And the droids were coming out …

'Put the explosives on the generator!' shouted Anakin. 'I'll fight these droids!'

As Anakin started to fight, Ahsoka took the explosives out of the bag.

* * *

Obi-Wan was a strong fighter, but he could not win against so many droids. When a big tank stopped in front of him, Obi-Wan knew the fight was over. A big blue head appeared from the top of the tank. It was General Loathsom, leader of the enemy. He gave Obi-Wan a terrible smile.

'I surrender,' the Jedi said. He pointed at a table and two chairs. 'The clone troopers will surrender too, but we must discuss how. Please sit down.'

Loathsom wasn't sure – maybe this was a trick? But he sat at the table.

'It is good to meet a famous enemy,' said Obi-Wan. But he was thinking, 'Hurry up, Anakin!'

* * *

'The explosives are ready!' shouted Ahsoka.

Anakin had his back to a wall and there were droids all around him.

Ahsoka looked at the building. There was a window above Anakin. Suddenly Ahsoka had an idea.

'Don't move!' she shouted.

Like all Jedi, Ahsoka could use the Force to move things. But this wall was very big … could she move it? She shut her eyes and tried very hard.

Anakin understood what she was going to do. 'No, no, no!' he shouted.

But then the wall fell, right on top of the droids around Anakin. The Jedi was OK because the open window fell over him.

'That wall almost killed me!' he shouted angrily.

* * *

Obi-Wan was still talking and Loathsom didn't like this. It was a trick!

He stood and ordered his droids, 'Get him!'

Obi-Wan jumped high in the air and hit two of the droids with the Force. Before the others could stop him, his arm was around Loathsom's neck. The droids were frightened to come closer.

Suddenly there was a loud sound from far away – KABOOM! Obi-Wan smiled.

'My friends have found the shield generator and destroyed it,' he said. 'Now more of the Republic army can come and help us.'

It was true. Obi-Wan could already see Republic ships over the city.

'It's over,' he told Loathsom. 'Tell your droids to put down their guns.'

'Surrender!' shouted Loathsom unhappily.

* * *

An hour later the Jedi were on a Republic ship above the planet. Yoda was with them. The little Jedi smiled up at Anakin.

'Problems with your new Padawan? Perhaps Obi-Wan can ...'

'No, it's OK!' answered Anakin quickly. 'She can stay with me.'

Yoda smiled to himself. He wanted this answer from Anakin.

'Then she will go with you to Teth,' said Yoda. 'Somebody has taken Jabba the Hutt's son there. You must find him.'

'Why has somebody taken Jabba's son?' asked Anakin. 'And why must we rescue him?'

'The Republic needs Jabba's help in the fight against Dooku,' said Obi-Wan.

Anakin wasn't happy. He hated Jabba – but he was a Jedi. He had to do this.

'Come on, Master, it doesn't sound hard,' said Ahsoka. 'I'll find Rex and the troops.'

She left.

'Don't worry, Anakin,' Obi-Wan smiled. 'Just teach her everything I taught you.'

'You know, I think this was your idea,' Anakin said to him.

Obi-Wan just smiled.

CHAPTER 3
Into the castle of the Hutt

Jabba the Hutt's castle was on the planet of Tatooine, far from Coruscant.

Obi-Wan was there to talk to him. 'We'll bring your son back,' the Jedi was saying.

'AHHH … WOWOGA SLEEMO MAKA PEEDUNKEE MUFKIN*' Jabba said angrily.

A language droid put Jabba's words into English for Obi-Wan: 'Who took my son? Bring that person back, too!'

Jabba looked down at Obi-Wan with cold, yellow eyes. 'You have one day to bring my son to me. After that, I will talk to Count Dooku. I'm sure he can help me …'

* * *

Anakin and Ahsoka were arriving at Teth. They were on one of five Republic ships, full of clone troopers.

Ahsoka looked out of the window. Behind the many trees, there was a long flat hill. There was a Hutt castle on the hill, but nobody lived in it now.

* Jabba speaks a different language.

'We think that Jabba's son, Rotta, is in that castle,' said Anakin.

'It won't be a problem,' said Ahsoka.

But suddenly there *was* a problem. BAM! Something was firing at the ships. BAM! BAM!

'Put the shields up!' Anakin shouted.

'Maybe this won't be so easy,' Ahsoka thought. She was a little frightened, but she didn't want to show it.

The ships landed and the doors opened.

'Go, go, go!' shouted Rex.

The clone troopers ran out, but something was still attacking them. Droids! They were firing down from the castle walls.

But Anakin had an idea. 'Use the Walkers!' he shouted.

Walkers were big tanks with six legs and big guns. They started to walk up the hill to attack the battle droids.

'Follow me!' Anakin shouted to Ahsoka.

He started to climb a wall, but Ahsoka had a better idea. She jumped onto one of the Walkers. Now she could ride to the top of the hill! BAM! Suddenly one of the droids hit the clone trooper on Ahsoka's Walker. The clone trooper fell, dead.

But Ahsoka's problems didn't stop there. Suddenly there were four droids in front of her. They were flying on special platforms. They started firing, but then Anakin jumped on to one of the platforms. The Jedi's lightsaber moved fast, then he pushed its droid off.

'Hurry up!' he shouted to Ahsoka with a smile.

Now Anakin was at the top of the wall, but the droids were waiting. They were all around him now.

'Surrender, Jedi!' shouted their leader.

Anakin was ready to fight, not surrender! Soon droid bodies were lying all around him. But then three new droids appeared. They were bigger and more dangerous – much more dangerous.

'Where are you, Ahsoka?' Anakin thought.

BOOM! Suddenly something hit the big droids.

Anakin turned and saw Ahsoka on top of the Walker.

'I'm here, Skyguy!' said his Padawan with a big smile.

Anakin smiled back. 'Finally you got here, Snips.'

'Just in time to rescue you,' Ahsoka laughed.

High up in the castle, somebody watched – and smiled.

* * *

Anakin and Ahsoka looked at all the destroyed droids outside the castle. Why were the droids here, on this little planet?

'It must be Dooku,' said Anakin. 'Let's find Rotta and go!'

Quickly they made a plan. The other clone troopers waited outside the castle. Anakin, Ahsoka, Rex and four troopers went through a small door into the castle. It was dark inside.

'I don't like this place,' said Rex.

Suddenly a droid appeared in the dark in front of them. It had a thin body and big eyes, like an insect.

'Who are you?' Anakin asked.

'I work at the castle,' answered the droid.

'Where is the young Hutt?' Anakin asked.

'The battle droids are keeping him in the room under the castle,' said the droid. 'But it is very dangerous. There are many droids in the castle.'

Anakin turned to Rex. 'Stay here with the troopers,' he said. 'Ahsoka and I will get the Hutt.'

As Anakin and Ahsoka walked down the stairs, the thin droid's big eyes watched them.

* * *

In another part of the castle, a woman in dark clothes walked into a secret room. This was Asajj Ventress. The Force was strong in her, but she was no Jedi – Ventress followed the dark side of the Force.

A hologram of Count Dooku appeared.

'Skywalker is inside the castle,' Ventress said. 'He is going now to rescue the Hutt.'

'Well done, Ventress,' said Dooku. 'The plan is working.'

Ventress smiled. She wasn't really interested in Dooku's plan. She cared about just one thing – she wanted to kill Anakin Skywalker.

* * *

'We're near the young Hutt now,' said Anakin.

'I know,' said Ahsoka. 'I can smell him!'

They opened a door and saw the little Hutt on the floor. Rotta looked like his father, but he was just a baby. The Hutt was crying.

'He's sweet!' said Ahsoka. 'What now?'

'You think he's sweet,' said Anakin, 'so you can carry him!'

Rotta wasn't big, but he was heavy. Ahsoka held him in both arms as she and Anakin went back to Rex.

The little Hutt was crying. Ahsoka put one hand on his head. 'He's very hot,' she told Anakin. 'I think he's ill.'

Anakin looked at Rotta. 'You're right,' he said. 'We must get him to the ship now!'

Anakin watched as Ahsoka put the little Hutt into a bag.

'I hate Hutts,' he said.

Anakin did not know it, but a droid was filming them.

* * *

A new guest was inside Jabba's castle on Tatooine.

'I have news about your son,' said Dooku. 'The Jedi took him! I've got proof.'

Dooku showed Jabba a film hologram from Teth. In the film, Ahsoka was putting Rotta into a bag. Anakin was watching and saying, 'I hate Hutts!'

When he heard these words, Jabba started shouting angrily.

'Don't worry,' said Dooku. 'My droids will rescue your son.' He gave a thin smile. 'And then maybe you will help us in our fight against the Republic …'

CHAPTER 4
An old enemy

Anakin and Ahsoka were standing with Rex and the troopers in an open area in the centre of the castle. R2D2 – Artoo – landed Anakin's Delta-7 ship next to them. A hologram of Obi-Wan appeared.

'Have you got Jabba's son?' Obi-Wan asked.

'Yes, but he's very ill,' Anakin said. 'He might die.'

'Anakin, you must get him back to Jabba alive. We need Jabba's help.'

Suddenly, some enemy fighters flew down to the castle and started firing at Rex and his men. A droid battleship pointed its guns at Anakin's ship – BAM! – and hit it. Artoo jumped out just in time.

'We're under attack!' Anakin shouted.

'I'll get there as soon as possible,' Obi-Wan said. 'Keep Rotta safe.'

Anakin looked down the hill. Maybe they could escape that way? No! An army of battle droids was coming up the hill. Escape was impossible!

'Go inside!' Anakin shouted.

When they were behind the castle door, Ahsoka looked

at her teacher. "What are we going to do? I think Rotta is really ill!'

'Do you have a plan, Snips?' Anakin asked.

Ahsoka smiled. 'Yes, but I need Artoo's help.'

BEEP! The little droid was saying 'yes'.

'Rex, try to stop the droids for as long as possible,' Anakin said. 'We have to find a way out.'

* * *

Minutes later, Anakin, Ahsoka and Artoo ran into a big room in the centre of the castle. Artoo went to the computer there. He fitted a thin arm from the centre of his body into the computer.

'Artoo will find a way out,' said Ahsoka.

Anakin looked at the Hutt in the bag on Ahsoka's back. Rotta was asleep now.

'Put him down and have some rest,' Anakin said. 'It's been a long day.'

'I'm not tired,' answered Ahsoka.

Anakin was angry. 'Why don't you listen?'

'I want to show you,' answered Ahsoka, 'that I'm not too young to be your Padawan.'

Anakin put his hand on the girl's arm. 'A Jedi once told me something – nothing happens by accident. You are my Padawan because the Force wants you to be.'

Suddenly there was a sound from another part of the castle. 'The battle droids are inside,' cried Anakin. 'We haven't got much time.'

BEEP! Artoo showed them a hologram map of the back of the castle.

'There's a landing platform at the back!' cried Anakin. 'We can call for a ship when we get there. Let's go.'

Suddenly they could hear Captain Rex on Anakin's

radio. 'Anakin, we're winning against the droids,' he said.

But Anakin didn't answer. He could feel the Force – something wasn't right. 'That's not like Rex,' he said to Ahsoka.

'Where are you now?' Rex asked.

Suddenly Anakin understood – it wasn't Rex.

'Ventress!' he cried. He could feel her dark energy now. 'She's here to kill Rotta,' he said. 'But Dooku will tell Jabba that the Jedi killed Rotta! Then Jabba will help Dooku. That's their plan!'

Anakin was right. Moments later, Ventress walked into the room with a group of battle droids. She had a lightsaber in each hand.

'How nice to see you again, Anakin! And you've got a pet now.'

'I'm no pet,' said Ahsoka.

Ventress said nothing. She ran at Anakin with her two lightsabers.

'Ahsoka, the droids!' shouted Anakin.

While Ahsoka fought the battle droids, Anakin faced Ventress.

'Surrender now!' he cried.

The dark side of the Force was strong in Ventress. Finally, she used it to push Anakin back to the wall. Anakin's body hit the wall hard, and he dropped his lightsaber.

'Get ready to die, Jedi!' said Ventress.

She lifted her lightsaber, but suddenly Ahsoka jumped on her back. Ventress turned and threw the girl to the floor.

But now Anakin's lightsaber was in his hand again.

'Get Rotta out of here,' he shouted to his Padawan.

Ahsoka ran to a door and opened it. A big hand appeared from the other side of the door.

Ahsoka looked up, frightened. 'Not good …'

Something ran in. It was very big and strong with teeth like knives.

'ROOOOOOOOWWRR!'

It was a rancor*, and it was dangerous and angry. It attacked Ahsoka. Quickly she moved her lightsaber up and hit the rancor on the nose. It fell on top of Ventress!

Was she dead? Anakin didn't wait to find out. 'Let's go!' he shouted.

A moment later, they heard the rancor's cry.

'Ventress isn't done with us yet,' thought Anakin. 'She won't stop until she kills me.'

They were at the platform now.

'Ahsoka, you were a great Jedi today,' Anakin said.

'Thank you, Master,' Ashoka said. Then she smiled. 'You know, Skyguy, that wasn't so difficult.'

But Anakin just said, 'We're not out of this yet.'

* A rancor is an animal from the planet Teth.

CHAPTER 5
Fly away!

Ahsoka looked at Rotta. 'He's really sick,' she said.

Suddenly there was a sound behind them. Two big battle droids were coming towards them. Ventress was behind them, with her lightsabers in her hands.

'Artoo, the door!' Anakin cried.

Artoo was next to a wall computer. A moment later, a big door came down, just in front of Ventress. But it could not stop her for long.

'She's cutting through the door with her lightsabers!' cried Ahsoka.

'We need to leave!' said Anakin.

But where? They were on a platform outside the castle. Anakin looked over the edge. Battle droids were climbing up the wall. They fired up at the platform and a group of big insects from the planet flew up into the sky, frightened.

Anakin looked back. Ventress was still cutting through the door. They didn't have much time …

Suddenly Rotta started to cry out.

'Not now!' said Ahsoka.

But the little Hutt didn't stop. He was excited about something.

'What is it?' asked Ahsoka.

Then she saw what he was pointing at – a second hill behind the castle, with another platform … and a ship!

'Look!' she cried.

There was just one problem. 'How can we get there?' asked Ahsoka.

Anakin smiled. 'Leave that to me.'

Then he ran at the edge of the platform and jumped off! A moment later he appeared again, and now he was riding on one of the big insects!

'I hope I don't have to do that!' said Ahsoka.

Artoo made a little sound that meant: 'Me too!'

But there was another sound behind them. It was Ventress! She was through the door, and she and her droids were running towards them. Ahsoka was ready to fight, but Ventress was too strong. She kicked the Padawan down. One of her lightsabers was just above the young girl.

'Where is Skywalker?' she cried. 'Tell me!'

'Here!' said Anakin, and he flew the insect right at Ventress. POW! The next moment, she was down.

Anakin put out his hand to Ahsoka, 'Come on, Snips!'

He pulled her up on to the insect with him. Artoo flew after them as Anakin pointed the insect at the second hill.

That ship was their only hope …

* * *

Obi-Wan was at Teth now, in a small battleship. After a hard fight with the flying droids, he landed on the platform near the castle.

But where was Anakin?

'Into the castle,' shouted Obi-Wan to the clone troopers.

On the other landing platform Anakin and Ahsoka could see the ship more easily. It was very old. It was difficult to read the name on its side: *Twilight*.

Ahsoka couldn't believe her eyes. 'We're leaving in *that*? That big insect was better …'

Anakin didn't say anything, but he wasn't sure about the *Twilight* either.

Ahsoka opened the door to the ship. The droid with big eyes – the one from the castle – was standing there. He was surprised to see them.

'What are you doing here?' asked Ahsoka.

'I … I ran away from the droids at the castle … '

A battle droid appeared behind him. 'Everything's on the ship,' it said. 'Let's go.'

Suddenly, Ahsoka understood – the droid was lying! He worked for Ventress!

But now more battle droids were running out of the ship. Angrily, Ahsoka waved her lightsaber. One, two, three battle droids fell.

Then there was only the droid with big eyes.

'Don't come near me!' he ordered.

Ahsoka's lightsaber moved fast and then – BANG! – The droid's head fell to the floor.

Anakin smiled and carried the baby Hutt on to the ship.

* * *

The fight in the castle wasn't going well for Captain Rex and his troopers. There were too many battle droids. Soon they were all around Rex and his men.

'You cannot win,' one of the droids said. 'Surrender, Republic dogs!'

But Rex did not surrender because suddenly a little ship appeared above them. Someone jumped out of it and landed in the centre of the battle droids. Obi-Wan Kenobi!

CHAPTER 6
Obi-Wan and Ventress

While Obi-Wan hit at the battle droids with his lightsaber, more Republic ships fired at them from the skies.

'Where's Skywalker?' Obi-Wan asked as they fought.

'He's probably still in the castle,' answered Rex.

'I'll go and find him,' said Obi-Wan. 'You stay with the droids!'

* * *

Inside the castle, Ventress was talking to Count Dooku on a holoprojector.

'Have you got Jabba's son yet?' asked Dooku's hologram.

A dark cloud passed across Ventress's face.

'Skywalker has the child,' she answered, 'but he will not escape from Teth.'

'We need Jabba's help,' Dooku said angrily. 'And for that, we need Jabba's son.'

'I understand,' said Ventress.

'Good,' said Dooku darkly. Then the hologram disappeared.

Angrily, Ventress turned away. Then she saw that she was not alone. Obi-Wan was standing at the door.

'Kenobi! You're always running after Skywalker,' Ventress said. Then she shouted to her super battle droids, 'Get him!'

As the droids closed around Obi-Wan, Ventress ran for the door. Anakin was a strong Jedi, but Obi-Wan was even stronger. She didn't want to fight him.

But Obi-Wan destroyed the droids quickly and ran after Ventress into a dark room.

'I know you're here, Ventress!' he cried. 'You can't hide!'

Suddenly Ventress ran out of the dark with her two lightsabers. Obi-Wan moved fast, but not fast enough. His lightsaber fell to the floor.

Ventress smiled. 'Now you die!'

* * *

Anakin was surprised – the *Twilight* was up in the skies of Teth! They flew over the castle.

'Rex needs our help,' said Anakin.

But Ahsoka put her hand on little Rotta's head. It was hotter now. 'Master, Rotta is worse,' she said. 'We can't let him die. We have to get him to a doctor on the big Jedi ship.'

Ahsoka was right. Anakin flew the *Twilight* up through the clouds – and right into the centre of a big battle.

One of Dooku's battleships was firing on the Jedi ship. Smaller fighters were flying around it, too. Three of the droid fighters saw the *Twilight* and started to fly towards it, instead.

Suddenly – BAM! – the Jedi ship started to fire at the *Twilight*, too.

'They think that we're the enemy!'

'Don't fire!' Anakin shouted into his radio.

But the droid fighters were still firing at them from behind.

'We can't land on our ship in this battle!' Anakin said. 'We must change our plan. We're going to take the *Twilight* all the way to Tatooine.'

He tried to go faster, but nothing happened. The ship was just too old and too slow.

'We can't get away from those droid fighters!' Anakin said. 'We'll never get into hyperspace*.'

Suddenly he had an idea. 'The ship is too heavy! Open the back doors, Ahsoka. Throw out anything we don't need!'

Ahsoka put Rotta down and ran to the back part of the ship. It was full of big boxes. She opened the back doors. Suddenly the *Twilight* began to climb and Ahsoka almost

* To travel between stars very quickly, a ship has to go into hyperspace.

fell out! Ahsoka was in terrible danger. The boxes were falling out, but she was holding onto the door – just.

'Don't be frightened,' she told herself. 'Frightened people make mistakes.'

Suddenly she had an idea. With one hand she took out her lightsaber.

'One, two, three …' She threw the lightsaber at the little computer on the wall. CLICK! The doors started to close.

When she came back, she said, 'It wasn't easy, but I did it.'

'You did it the hard way,' said Anakin. 'You can open and close the back doors with the computer right here!'

The ship was almost going fast enough now.

Anakin looked down at Rotta. 'Don't die,' he said to the little Hutt.

Then the *Twilight* jumped into hyperspace.

* * *

On Teth, Ventress's lightsabers moved fast, but Obi-Wan moved faster. He jumped up and held her hands in his. The two enemies were face to face.

'Hello,' he said.

He pushed her back and picked up his lightsaber.

'We know about Dooku's plan,' he said as the battle continued.

'His plan will work when you die!' shouted Ventress.

But Obi-Wan understood something – sometimes it was better not to fight. He ran to an open window and jumped out.

'You can't run!' shouted Ventress.

But Obi-Wan was smiling as he stood on the wall outside the window.

Suddenly both he and Ventress felt something – a

change in the Force. They looked up at the skies.

'Anakin has left Teth,' Obi-Wan said. 'You have lost!'

But Ventress wasn't ready to surrender yet. At that moment a droid fighter flew past the castle window and she jumped on to it.

Obi-Wan could only watch as his enemy flew away.

* * *

Dooku was very angry when he heard the news about Anakin. But his plan could still work. He went back to see Jabba.

'I have bad news,' said Dooku. 'The Jedi killed your son. Now Skywalker is coming here to kill *you*.'

'JEDI SLEEMO!' Jabba cried.

'Don't worry, great Jabba. We will kill Skywalker when he lands.'

Jabba agreed. This was a good ending for a Jedi dog, like Skywalker.

Dooku smiled as he left. 'Ventress has failed, but I will not,' he thought. 'I will kill the young Hutt and then destroy Skywalker.'

CHAPTER 7
Home to Tatooine

Anakin and Ahsoka could see planet Tatooine below them.

'Welcome home, Skyguy,' Ahsoka said.

But Anakin wasn't happy at all. 'I never wanted to see this place again.'

'OK … what happened?' Ahsoka asked.

'I don't want to talk about it.'

When Anakin was a child, he lived on Tatooine. It was a hard and difficult time for him. For years, someone owned him there – that person was Jabba the Hutt. 'How's Rotta?' he asked.

'He's better now,' Ahsoka said.

Suddenly, two battle ships appeared.

'Someone wants to kill Rotta,' Anakin said.

BAM! The ships fired – and hit the *Twilight*! BAM!

'Hang on! I'm going to land, but it isn't going to be soft,' Anakin cried.

BANG! The *Twilight* landed on Tatooine.

* * *

On Coruscant, Padmé Amidala was in the office of Chancellor Palpatine. She was once the Queen of Naboo; now she was a Senator for the Republic.

'I have heard there are battles in the far parts of the Republic,' she said.

'Yes,' answered Palpatine. 'Kenobi and Skywalker were in a fight.'

'Anakin?' said Padmé. 'Is he in danger?'

'Jabba thinks that Anakin took his son,' said Palpatine.

Padmé knew that Jabba was wrong.

'Jabba has an uncle here on Coruscant,' she said. 'I can go and talk to him.'

'Be careful,' said Palpatine as she walked to the door. 'The Hutts are dangerous.'

But Padmé knew that she must try. Padmé and Anakin were in love. They could not be together – she was once a queen and he was a Jedi. But they married in secret a few months ago.

* * *

Soon, Padmé was outside Ziro the Hutt's castle. She followed a house droid inside.

Ziro was even fatter than Jabba.

'I am Senator Amidala,' Padmé said.

'How can I help?' he asked.

'You are Jabba's uncle. Jabba thinks the Jedi have taken his son,' she said. 'I can explain everything. The Jedi have rescued his son.'

Ziro didn't want to listen. 'Take her out!'

A battle droid with a gun took Padmé out of the room.

'No!' thought Padmé. 'Anakin is still in danger!'

She turned and kicked the gun out of the battle droid's hand. Then she ran back to Ziro's room. But Ziro did not see her. He was talking to a hologram of Count Dooku.

'We've got problems,' Ziro said. 'A Senator from the Republic was here! Maybe she'll find out that I helped you to take Jabba's son.'

'Don't worry,' said Dooku. 'Jabba thinks the Jedi have already killed his son. He thinks Skywalker is coming to kill him.'

'Jabba will kill him first!' said Ziro.

'Yes. And when that happens, you will be leader of all the Hutts.'

'But what about Senator Amidala?'

'Maybe she will have a little accident,' said Dooku.

Padmé suddenly understood that she was in real danger here. She turned to run, but it was too late. A droid was behind her. It pulled her into the centre of the room.

Padmé gave the hologram of Dooku a cold look. 'I see that the enemy of the Republic is back again.'

'Ziro, some of the Republic's enemies will pay a lot of money for Senator Amidala,' Dooku said.

Ziro's mouth opened in a big smile. 'Take her to the bottom of the castle,' he ordered his droids.

'You'll be sorry!' shouted Padmé, but Ziro just laughed.

'No, I'll be rich!'

* * *

'Jabba's castle is that way,' Anakin said. 'We must hurry.'

They started walking. Anakin didn't speak. Ahsoka knew that he was thinking about his early years on this planet.

Suddenly Anakin stopped. Something was wrong. Ahsoka could feel it too – a change in the Force.

'It's the dark side of the Force,' Anakin said, 'and it's coming for Rotta.'

He gave Ahsoka a long look. 'Listen,' he said. 'We can't stay together. Here's the plan …'

CHAPTER 8
The plan

With four battle droids outside the room, there was no way for Padmé to escape.

Suddenly her holoprojector made a sound. 'What's that?' said one of the droids.

Padmé began to hope. 'Don't touch that!' she shouted. 'Please! You mustn't touch it!'

Her trick worked: one of the droids picked the holoprojector up. A hologram of Padmé's language droid C-3PO – Threepio – appeared.

'You answered! I've been so worried,' Threepio cried. Then he saw the battle droid. 'Wait! Who are you? You're not Padmé.'

Padmé knew that she didn't have much time. 'Threepio, get help!' she shouted. 'I'm in Ziro's castle!'

'You're in trouble! I knew it!' Threepio cried.

A moment later the droid threw the holoprojector to the floor and broke it.

'Did Threepio hear me?' Padmé asked herself. She could only wait and see …

* * *

Anakin saw a little cloud just above the land. It was far away but it was coming closer.

It was Count Dooku on an air bike.

Dooku pointed at the bag on Anakin's back. 'Give me the little Hutt or die!' he ordered. He fired Sith energy at Anakin from his hands. The Jedi hit it away with his lightsaber.

'Ha! Be ready to die, boy,' said Dooku.

The two started to fight with their lightsabers, but Dooku wasn't trying to hit Anakin. Suddenly he jumped around and hit the bag on Anakin's back. It fell into two pieces.

'I have won!' smiled Dooku. 'Jabba's son is dead!'

But Anakin smiled too. 'Look again!'

Dooku looked at the bag – the little Hutt's body wasn't in there. The bag was full of rocks – a trick!

'Rotta is with my Padawan,' said Anakin. 'They're almost at Jabba's castle now.'

* * *

Ahsoka could see Jabba's castle. Little Rotta could see it too, and the baby was very happy.

'We're almost there,' Ahsoka told Artoo.

But suddenly three super battle droids came out of the castle. Ahsoka took out her lightsaber and waited for the fight to start.

* * *

'Your little trick isn't important,' said Dooku coldly. 'My droids will kill Jabba's son and then they'll take your Padawan to Jabba. He won't be kind.'

Dooku lifted his lightsaber. He was ready to fight until Anakin was dead. But Anakin had other ideas. He ran to Dooku's air bike. Before his enemy could do anything, Anakin was riding away.

'I'm coming, Ahsoka!' he thought.

* * *

Ziro's angry yellow eyes were on Padmé.

'My droids tell me that you called for help,' he said. 'You are too dangerous. It will be much easier to kill you …'

BOOM!

'Explosives!' shouted Ziro. 'But who is attacking us?'

The answer came quickly as Republic clone troopers ran into the room, with Threepio! The troopers started to fire at Ziro's droids.

Ziro tried to escape, but he was too big and slow. Padmé had a gun in her hand now. She pointed it at him and smiled. 'Stop right there, Ziro!'

* * *

Ahsoka was still fighting the droids outside Jabba's castle. One of them was down, but the other two were still dangerous.

Suddenly Ahsoka heard a sound. She looked up and saw an air bike with Anakin on it!

'Master! Over here!' she shouted, but Anakin didn't stop.

'He never listens!' Ahsoka said. She looked angrily at the two battle droids. 'You're going back to Jabba in little pieces now.'

Inside the castle, the Hutt's language droid said, 'Anakin Skywalker is here. And Count Dooku was right – your son is not with him.'

Anakin looked around. 'What? Your son isn't here yet? Then where is my Padawan?'

Jabba started to shout angrily. But Anakin did not wait for the language droid to explain the Hutt's words. He ran at Jabba and pointed his lightsaber at him.

'What have you done with my Padawan?' Anakin said angrily.

Jabba said something.

'He says that you came here to kill him,' said the language droid.

'I came here to explain everything,' said Anakin.

The droid put Jabba's answer into Anakin's language: 'You came here to die.'

Anakin looked around the room. There were a lot of Jabba's fighters here, from many different planets, all very dangerous. Could he fight them all and win? He didn't know. But he was ready to try.

'Stop!'

Anakin looked around. Ahsoka was at the door. She was tired and dirty, but she was smiling. And she had Rotta! The little baby was sleeping happily.

Jabba looked from his son to the two Jedi. He said something in his language.

'Jabba says that now you both must die,' said the droid.

'WHAT?'

Anakin and Ahsoka's lightsabers were ready, as their enemies moved closer.

'Does this always happen to you?' asked Ahsoka.

'Everywhere I go,' said Anakin.

But suddenly there was a sound from Jabba's holoprojector.

'Your uncle Ziro is sending a message,' said the language droid.

When the hologram appeared, it wasn't Ziro – it was Padmé.

'Jabba!' she cried. 'Your uncle is part of a terrible plan against you.'

A hologram of Ziro appeared next to her.

Padmé continued, 'Ziro helped Dooku to take your son. They wanted you to think that the Jedi did it.'

Jabba was angrier than ever before.

The language droid said, 'The Hutt family will decide on Ziro's future.'

Now Padmé said, 'Maybe now you will let the Republic's ships use Hutt air space?'

Jabba thought about this for a moment.

'Jabba agrees,' said the language droid.

Anakin looked up at the hologram of Padmé and said, 'Senator Amidala … Thank you.'

Padmé smiled at him. 'No, Anakin. I, and the Republic, thank *you*.'

The two looked at each other for a moment … perhaps a moment too long. Ahsoka watched them.

'That's strange,' she thought. 'Another thing I don't know about the Master.'

Then the hologram of Padmé Amidala disappeared.

* * *

Count Dooku didn't like sending a hologram message with bad news to Darth Sidious.

'The plan did not work,' said Dooku. 'Jabba will let the Republic use Hutt air space. Our fight has become more difficult.'

It was impossible to see Darth Sidious's face inside his dark clothes. But his voice came deep and clear. 'Don't worry, my friend. We can let the Jedi win this one small battle. In the end, we will win!'

* * *

Anakin and Ahsoka waited for a Republic ship outside Jabba's castle.

Ahsoka felt happy as she looked at the Jedi by her side. When she went to study at the Jedi Temple, her biggest dream was to become a Jedi Knight. Now that dream seemed closer than ever.

THE STAR WARS STORY

When George Lucas wanted to make *Star Wars* in the early 1970s, some people in Hollywood were not sure about an adventure film in space. They were wrong: people around the world *loved* the film. 'I was the most surprised of anybody,' says Lucas. Now, there are six films – and a new part of the story – *The Clone Wars.*

EPISODE I: The Phantom Menace (1999)

Obi-Wan Kenobi and his Jedi teacher rescue the queen of Naboo, Padmé Amidala. Then on Tatooine they find a young boy, Anakin Skywalker. The Force is very strong in Anakin.

When they return to Naboo, they learn that the Sith – a group that follows the dark side of the Force – are back.

EPISODE II: Attack of the Clones (2002)

Ten years later, Obi-Wan is now a Jedi teacher. Anakin is his student, but he has become very strong. They must save Padmé from enemies of the Republic. Anakin and Padmé fall in love – but their love is a secret.

EPISODE III: Revenge of the Sith (2005)

The Republic ends and the Empire begins. Jedi Anakin Skywalker joins the dark side of the force. His name is now Darth Vader.

With many other Jedi dead, Obi-Wan and Yoda must hide. But there is hope – Anakin's children are born in secret. They are Luke Skywalker and Princess Leia.

STAR WARS: The Clone Wars (2008)

The Clone Wars comes between episodes two and three of the Star Wars story. It is an animated film. As their enemies become stronger, Anakin and Obi-Wan must fight to save the Republic.

Revenge of the Sith

EPISODE IV: A New Hope (1977)

On the planet of Tatooine, young Luke Skywalker knows nothing about his parents. He meets Obi-Wan Kenobi and helps him to rescue Princess Leia. Obi-Wan dies, but Luke learns that the Force is strong in him. He uses it to destroy the Empire's terrible new weapon, the Death Star.

EPISODE V: The Empire Strikes Back (1980)

Three years later, the Empire is trying to destroy all its enemies. Luke studies to be a Jedi with Yoda. He faces Darth Vader in battle. Vader wants Luke to join the dark side of the Force - then Luke finds out Darth Vader is his father!

EPISODE VI: Return of the Jedi (1983)

This is the final battle between the Empire and its enemies. Luke faces his father again, this time in front of the Emperor. Darth Vader destroys the Emperor and saves his son. Darth Vader – Anakin Skywalker – dies too, but the Republic is free again.

What do you think? Have you seen any *Star Wars* films? If so, which ones? Which *Star Wars* films would you like to see? Why?

What do these words mean? You can use a dictionary.
episode animated empire Emperor death weapon

STAR WARS:

We hear the name in the very first film, but we don't find out anything more about the Clone Wars until much later. Film-maker Dave Filoni saw the first *Star Wars* film when he was a boy. He saw that there was another story – a story that wasn't in the films.

Now, Filoni is helping to write that story in *The Clone Wars*. But this film is very different from the other *Stars Wars* films: the film-makers have used computers to make an animated film. They are also making a television series with the same characters. In fact, the idea for the TV series came first.

IN THEIR WORDS

George Lucas:

‘This film happened by accident. We were making an animated television series. But when I saw the first parts, I thought, "*This is fantastic! People need to see this in a cinema!*"’

Actor Matt Lanter (the voice of Anakin):

‘In the other *Star Wars* films, Anakin is a dark character. But that's not what you see in *Clone Wars*. He likes to have fun and joke with Obi-Wan and Ahsoka.’

Actress Ashley Eckstein (the voice of Ahsoka):

‘I think we *really* need an Ahsoka character right now – she shows that girls can win.’

THE CLONE WARS

HELLO, OLD FRIENDS …

Two of the most popular characters in the first *Star Wars* film were the droids, C-3PO and R2-D2. These two very different droids are back in *The Clone Wars*.

In fact, Anthony Daniels, the voice of C-3PO, is one of only two actors who appears in all of the *Star Wars* films. 'I've now played C-Threepio for over half my life!' says the British actor.

R2-D2 and C-3PO

Dave Filoni (film-maker of *The Clone Wars*):

'We wanted the film to be exciting and sometimes funny. We don't want to forget to have fun. George was very clear about that.'

George Lucas:

'You can do much more in a TV series. In a film, we can have a funny character in the story for eight seconds, but I can't tell their story. In a series, I can do that. It's a little lighter … more fun.'

George Lucas

"You fought in the Clone Wars?"

Luke Skywalker to Obi-Wan Kenobi, in *A New Hope*.

What do you think?
Who is your favourite character in *The Clone Wars?* Why?

What do these words mean? You can use a dictionary.
character robot animated series voice actor

SPACE EXPLORATION

In *The Clone Wars* people travel through space to and from different planets and stars. They meet people from other planets. But what about real life? How much have we explored space already? Will people ever travel to or live on other stars?

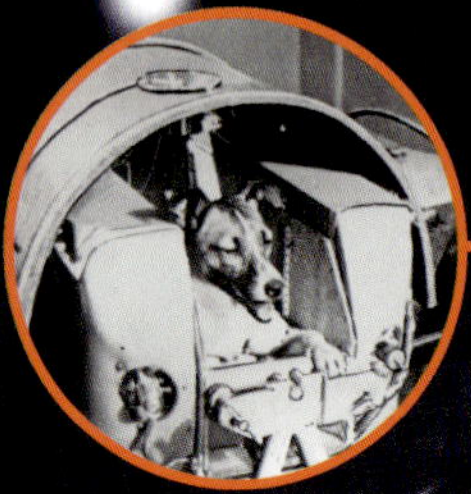

The history of space exploration

- **1957:** Soviet scientists send the **satellite** Sputnik into space and around our planet, the Earth.
- **1957-58:** The first animals go into space.
- **1961:** Russian astronaut Yuri Gagarin becomes the first man in space.
- **1969:** American astronaut Neil Armstrong is the first man on the moon.
- **1971:** The Soviet Union puts the first space station in space.
- **1983:** Sally Ride becomes the first American woman in space.
- **1998:** The International Space Station (ISS) begins. Astronauts can live in space.
- **2001:** Space tourism begins: non-astronauts can go into space for the first time.
- **2002:** Robots start to explore Mars.
- **2004:** A satellite takes photographs of Saturn's rings.
- **2008:** Scientists study how people can live and work in space for longer.

What do these words mean? You can use a dictionary.

explore / exploration satellite space tourism scientist astronaut ice gravity

ASK THE SPACE SCIENTIST!

Here are the answers to some popular questions about space exploration.

What are the problems for people in space?

In space, there is no gravity. People can fly slowly through the air. Everyday life is difficult – eating, drinking, sleeping and going to the bathroom all have their own problems!

About half of all astronauts feel ill for their first few days in space.

How far away are other planets and stars?

When astronauts first went to the moon, it took three days to reach it. But Earth's closest neighbour is the planet Venus. Venus is 40,000,000 kilometres away – 100 times further than the moon!

Scientists do not talk about travel to other stars in kilometres. They say how many light years a star is from us. A light year is how far light can travel in one year. Proxima Centauri, the nearest star to our sun, is 4.2 light years away – it takes light over four years to travel between the two stars.

Is there life on other planets?

Nobody has ever stood on another planet, but robot ships from Earth *have* explored other planets around our sun. These robots have sent back important information to scientists on Earth.

In 2002 the Mars Explorer discovered a lot of ice in one part of Mars. This was very exciting. If there is ice, there was once water. Water is very important for life. So maybe there was once life on Mars ...

A model of the Mars Explorer.

What will happen in the future?

Perhaps people will go back to the moon again - and even build a station there. Astronauts may even go to Mars.

What do you think?
Will people from Earth ever live on other planets? Why / Why not?

PROLOGUE-CHAPTER 2

Before you read

You can use a dictionary.

1 Complete the sentences with these words.

air space attack battle cut cut off destroyed enemy explosives generator surrender weak

a) 'Put your hands up and ...!' shouted the police.
b) Many people on both sides died in the ... that day.
c) 'Be careful! There are ... in that bag!'
d) 'Our army is strong. We can defeat their army. They are ...'
e) A ... makes light and heat for our house.
f) 'We have no home! The storm ... our house!'
g) The droids started to ... the Jedi Knights.
h) You can ... the cake with a knife.
i) The ... fired at our men with guns.
j) Obi-wan ... the droid's arm.
k) 'That country's army will fire at you, if you fly through their ...'

2 Use these words to answer the questions.

air army battleship energy hologram insect leader planet shield space war

a) Where are the stars?
b) What fights for a country?
c) What goes around a sun?
d) What can you see but not hold?
e) What is a fight between two countries?
f) What keeps a person or thing safe?
g) What has six legs?
h) Where do birds fly?
i) Who gives orders?
j) What do cars and cities use a lot of?
k) What fights in the air or at sea?

3 Look at 'People and Places' on pages 4–7. Answer the questions. Who ...

a) ... is learning to be a Jedi Knight?

- **b)** ... was once a queen?
- **c)** ... is over 800?
- **d)** . . . fights with two lightsabers?
- **e)** . . . is Rotta's father?
- **f)** . . . can speak over six million languages?

After you read

4 Are these sentences true or false? Correct the false sentences.

- **a)** The Jedi Temple is on the planet Christophsis.
- **b)** Count Dooku wants to keep the Republic safe.
- **c)** The Jedi send Ahsoka with a message for Anakin and Obi-Wan.
- **d)** Ahsoka is going to be Obi-Wan's student.
- **e)** Anakin and Ahsoka destroy the shield generator.
- **f)** General Loathsom surrenders to Obi-Wan.
- **g)** Jabba the Hutt is an old friend of Anakin's.

CHAPTERS 3–5

Before you read

5 In Chapter 3 Anakin and Ahsoka are *under attack*. What are they under attack from? Choose the correct answer. (You can use a dictionary.)

a) clones **b)** enemy droids **c)** Jabba the Hutt

6 Which is which?

castle platform

a) The king lived in a .... **b)** The speaker stood on a ... .

After you read

7 Put these parts of the story in order.

- **a)** Artoo joins Anakin.
- **b)** A rancor (a big animal from Teth) attacks Anakin and Ahsoka.
- **c)** Anakin and Ahsoka go into the Hutt castle on Teth.
- **d)** Anakin and Ahsoka arrive on Teth.
- **e)** Anakin and Ventress fight with lightsabers.
- **f)** Obi-Wan visits Jabba on Tatooine.
- **g)** Count Dooku lies to Jabba the Hutt.
- **h)** Anakin and Ahsoka find Rotta, the little Hutt.

CHAPTERS 6-8

Before you read

8 What do you think?

a) Obi-Wan and Ventress fight. Who wins?

b) Who is waiting for Anakin and Ahsoka on Tatooine. Why?

After you read

9 Circle the correct answer.

a) What can't the *Twilight* land on?
i) the planet of Tatooine **ii)** the Jedi ship **iii)** Jabba's castle

b) Why doesn't Ventress surrender to Obi-Wan?
i) She flew away on a droid fighter. **ii)** She won the fight. **iii)** Her army of droids arrived.

c) Who does Padmé go to see?
i) Jabba the Hutt ii) Jabba's son **iii)** Jabba's uncle

d) Why does Dooku hit the bag on Anakin's back?
i) to kill Anakin **ii)** to kill Rotta **iii)** to trick Anakin

e) Why does help arrive for Padmé?
i) Chancellor Palpatine sends help. **ii)** Her language droid hears her message for help. **iii)** She escapes from Ziro's castle and calls for help.

10 Complete the sentences with these names.

Ahsoka Anakin Dooku Obi-Wan Padmé

a) ... Nobody knows that she is Anakin's wife.

b) ... He tells Ventress that she has lost.

c) ... Somebody takes his air bike.

d) ... She throws boxes out of the *Twilight*.

e) ... He tricks Dooku with a bag of rocks.

11 What do you think?

a) What will Dooku and Ventress do next?

b) Which of the people in the story are going to move to the dark side of the Force?